TURTLES
KW-051

Contents

Photography: Dr. Herbert R. Axelrod; Patrick Burchfield: Isabelle Francaise; Michael Gilroy; Bob Gossington; A. Jesse; Burkhard Kahl; Bruce Major; Dr. Sherman Minton; A van den Nieuwenhuizen; Dr. Peter Pritchard; P. Schauenberg; Vince Serbin; Sally Anne Thompson. **Colored drawings:** R. & D. Zinck; John R. Quinn.

Distributed in the UNITED STATES by T.F.H. Publications, Inc., One T.F.H. Plaza, Neptune City, NJ 07753; in CANADA to the Pet Trade by H & L Pet Supplies Inc., 27 Kingston Crescent, Kitchener, Ontario N2B 2T6; Rolf C. Hagen Ltd., 3225 Sartelon Street, Montreal 382 Quebec; in CANADA to the Book Trade by Macmillan of Canada (A Division of Canada Publishing Corporation), 164 Commander Boulevard, Agincourt, Ontario M1S 3C7; in ENGLAND by T.F.H. Publications Limited, Cliveden House/Priors Way/Bray, Maidenhead, Berkshire SL6 2HP, England; in AUSTRALIA AND THE SOUTH PACIFIC by T.F.H. (Australia) Pty. Ltd., Box 149, Brookvale 2100 N.S.W., Australia; in NEW ZEALAND by Ross Haines & Son, Ltd., 18 Monmouth Street, Grey Lynn, Auckland 2, New Zealand; in SINGAPORE AND MALAYSIA by MPH Distributors (S) Pte., Ltd., 601 Sims Drive, #03/07/21, Singapore 1438; in the PHILIPPINES by Bio-Research, 5 Lippay Street, San Lorenzo Village, Makati Rizal; in SOUTH AFRICA by Multipet Pty. Ltd., 30 Turners Avenue, Durban 4001. Published by T.F.H. Publications, Inc. Manufactured in the United States of America by T.F.H. Publications, Inc.

TURTLES

Mervin F. Roberts

Preface

Many competently written natural history and animal care books wind up actually suffering from the type of effort their authors lavished on them.

On one hand, there are authors who aim for a simple story, simply told. To accomplish this, they generalize and lump the facts. These books suffer because living things thrive and multiply by virtue of their specialized habits.

On the other hand, there are those authors who try to catch every nuance of difference in behavior or appearance between genera, species, subspecies, races, and even varieties. All the known facts are presented. These books suffer because the reader is snowed under and loses sight of the big picture while struggling with inconsequential details.

Of course, I know this, so I tried to avoid both these pitfalls; I have attempted to simplify the story and still provide the details needed by pet keepers. Perhaps I did not completely succeed, but I did try. It was not easy. Without the help I got from my wife Edith (who typed the

The red-eared turtle, Pseudemys scripta elegans, *is probably the most widely kept reptile the world has ever seen. However, in the United States there are some restrictions in the sale of this turtle.*

Box turtles like this Terrapene ornata ornata *can make excellent pets, if their needs are given full consideration.*

manuscript) and Michael Klemens (who reviewed it) and Louis Porras and Joe Beraducci and Dr. Arthur R. English (who advised me) and Bruce Major (who made many of the photos) and William McFarland (who provided me with some turtles), there would be nothing. Suffice it to say, the mistakes are all mine.

Turtles As Pets was my first little book about pets. Dr. Herbert R. Axelrod commissioned it in 1954 and now, after a quarter of a century, he gave me the opportunity to go at it again. Why bother? That old 32-pager is still being read—

letters with comments still dribble in. But today pet keepers are more sophisticated. They want more useful facts, more pertinent details, more accurate reasons. Also, we have accumulated a great deal of information about these animals that wasn't known or wasn't considered important then. So here it is, completely re-written, with many more pages and many new pictures—and with more of the facts and details and reasons that you have been asking for.

Mervin Roberts
Old Lyme, Connecticut

Introduction

There are egg-laying mammals and birds that don't fly and snakes with footlike spurs and legless lizards and air-breathing fish and crustaceans that don't entirely molt—but when the cloth was cut for turtles, there were not too many loose threads. Because all turtles are reptiles they have a great deal in common with each other, of course—and, in terms of their appearance, not much in common with any other thing. No one should confuse a turtle with something else. True, some have hard shells and some have hinged shells and some have soft shells, but from where people stand, all turtles—and only turtles—have turtle-shaped shells.

All turtles are toothless. All have tails and eyelids, but no external ears or even ear openings, and most have no voice to speak of. In case you wondered about the famous verse from the Song of Songs 2:12, "The voice of the turtle is heard throughout the land," this passage is sometimes translated to read "turtle dove," and it refers to a pigeon. As a matter of fact, the turtle doesn't get any specific coverage anywhere in the Bible.

The Oxford English Dictionary devotes all of one and one-third pages to "turtle" and still another whole page to "tortoise."

TURTLE-KEEPING IN GENERAL

If you plan to keep turtles as pets, there are a few hazards you must be aware of. The first is tied to the diet of some terrestrial species. If a turtle that is accustomed to eating mushrooms (box turtles are good examples) consumes a poisonous mushroom and you eat the turtle, you could end up with mushroom poisoning. I know of only one

Wide spectrum antibiotics like Tetracycline are sold in most pet shops.

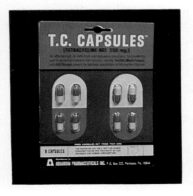

recorded instance in the history of mankind, so your risk is somewhat remote, but don't say I didn't warn you.

Another risk (this one potentially much greater) which accompanies the keeping of aquatic and semi-aquatic turtles is a disease called *Salmonella* infection, or salmonellosis, named after a public health microbiologist named Salmon. This disease is similar to typhoid fever but is less dangerous. It is best controlled by habitat cleanliness. It may be "cured" by antibiotics, but the real control should be at the habitat level. If water-loving turtles are kept in clean water which is changed frequently, the aerobic Gram-negative organisms which cause the disease will be carried away, and the fecal matter and decaying uneaten turtle food which these bacteria consume will be diluted to concentrations which will not support them. Bear in mind that these bacteria are present always and everywhere. It is their *concentration* that determines the degree of danger.

Salmonella infection is not

Clean water is a must for aquatic and semi-aquatic turtles in captivity. Outright removal of polluted water is the only means of reducing bacterial growth.

a "turtle disease." It can be transmitted by any polluted water regardless of the animal involved. My suggestion is that you rely on cleanliness and not on "wonder drugs" for protection. Bear in mind that the germs are *everywhere*. They accumulate in dangerous concentrations only where decaying food and fecal matter are available to feed them and the temperature and moisture

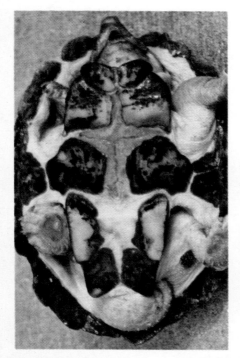

The upper shell covering of the turtle is called the carapace, the lower half is called the plastron. Both carapace and plastron can vary greatly in shape and markings from family to family among turtle species. (Left) Plastron of razorback-backed musk turtle; (below) carapace of juvenile red-eared turtle; and **facing page:** *the red-colored indicator points to the hinge of the plastron of an American box turtle.*

are suited to their needs. Still another hazard you should be aware of is the hazard of violating the law. Today, many species of turtles are protected by legislation or by administrative fiat, and to possess a protected animal may subject you to such penalty as the law may impose. For example, the ordinary common box turtle (*Terrapene carolina*) is protected in New York and some other states. Both the sale and the possession of this species in those states are prohibited—except to certain zoos.

Don't worry, the hobby is not seriously endangered yet. There are still plenty of unprotected species in plentiful supply, but as time goes on your freedom to collect and possess any wild animals will surely be progressively restricted. There are a variety of pressures and pressure groups working here. Taking a historical view, this is what must happen as human population increases and wild animal habitat is restricted.

So much for the hazards. On the bright side, turtles are all relatively quiet, at least some are easy to feed, most

are odorless, many are long-lived, pet turtles don't attack people—and no turtle is venomous. They are resistant to parasites and disease. With intelligent and humane care, your pet turtle will have a good chance of outliving you.

This book is intended primarily to be a pet care book and is organized with that aim in mind.

Regardless of whether you have a terrestrial species like a box turtle or a gopher tortoise or a semi-aquatic red-ear turtle or an almost completely aquatic species like a soft-shell or a snapping turtle, your turtle will be covered.

Each habitat will be considered separately along with a list of the commonly kept species and their special requirements in captivity. If you want to become involved with the natural history of these interesting creatures, you should read Pritchard or Pope or Carr or Ernst and Barbour; then join the Herpetologists League or American Society of Ichthyologists and Herpetologists or the Society for the Study of Amphibians and Reptiles (S.S.A.R.) and also a local herpetological society. Oftentimes a high school biology teacher or your pet shop proprietor will know who in your area is already active with turtles. You can get a lot of help from an established hobbyist—this is an on-going thing—and some day you may be called on to help another beginner. It's a challenge and it's fun!

Phylum: **Chordata**—the chordates have a central nervous system which is dorsally situated. The mollusks, arthropods, worms and some other groups drop off here.

American box turtle, Terrapene carolina, *may be found near water in the wild, enters very shallow waters of an inch or so in depth, and can swim but very poorly.*

TAXONOMY OF TURTLES

Kingdom: **Animalia**—the animals. The protozoa, fungi and plants are placed elsewhere. Some scientists lump the fungi and plants. They are known as lumpers. Some scientists split the fungi from the plants. These people are known as splitters.

Subphylum: **Vertebrata**—the vertebrate animals have a cartilage or bony spinal column which encloses at least part of the central nervous system. Some older texts rank **Vertebrata** as a phylum. Still other classifiers work in a category of **Craniata** for creatures which

The purchase of a pet turtle or intentional keeping of a captured wild turtle should not be taken lightly. The potential new turtle keeper should be prepared with the proper equipment and disposition. This young boy is starting off on the right foot with an all-glass aquarium as an enclosure for his pet box turtle. **Facing page:** Children receiving instruction in the rudiments of turtle care from an informed adult—in this case the author, their grandfather.

Introduction

have a brain case at the front end of the vertebral column.

Class: **Reptilia**—here are the reptiles. They differ from all other vertebrates with respect to the occipital bone. In reptiles there is a single occipital condyle (or bony process). In amphibians and mammals there are two of these bones at the base of the skull. Birds have but one (like reptiles); however, *they* have feathers (unlike reptiles). Fishes have no occipital bones. In the class of reptiles there are according to some but not all authorities about 5500 species.

Order: **Testudinata** or **Chelonia.** These names mean the same creatures. The former is preferred today. There are two suborders and twelve living families. These twelve living families are broken down into 66 genera and the genera into 221 species.

One suborder is Cryptodira. Cryptodiran turtles all withdraw their heads by bending the neck in the shape of the letter "S" in a *vertical* plane. Most turtles are in this suborder. They are found all over the temperate and tropical world.

Another suborder is Pleurodira. Pleurodirans withdraw their heads by turning them mostly in a *horizontal* plane. Call them side-neck turtles. All side-necks are found on the southern continents.

Families: There is no sense in going into this subject here. You should go directly to Dowling and Duellman or Pritchard.

Genera : As pet keepers, let's look at only those genera of turtles which are kept as pets and quickly pass over the difficult, delicate, expensive, rare and endangered species. You have no business keeping them no matter how you come by them.

Oh yes, Carr, Pritchard, Dowling and Duellman. These men are all classification specialists, and if you want specifics on identification you should first read Pritchard. For specifics on classification down to the family level, read Dowling and Duellman. For American species see Carr or Ernst and Barbour.

Pritchard, Peter C. H., *Encyclopedia of Turtles,* 1979. TFH Publications, Inc., Neptune, New Jersey.

Dowling, Herndon and
    Duellman, William E.,
    *Systematic Herpetology: A
    Synopsis of Families and
    Higher Categories,* 1978.
    HISS Publications.
Carr, Archie, *Handbook of
    Turtles,* 1952. Cornell
    University Press, Ithaca,
    N.Y.

SOME BIOLOGICAL CONSIDERATIONS

Odor

Turtles are sensitive to odors. They find their food mostly by its odor and odor may also assist a female as she searches for her nesting grounds. It is also very likely that sexy turtles can tell the boys from the girls by their odor.

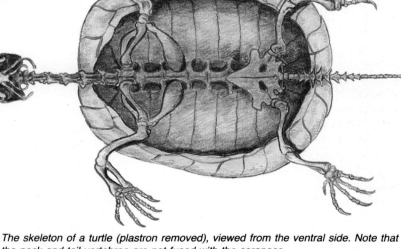

The skeleton of a turtle (plastron removed), viewed from the ventral side. Note that the neck and tail vertebrae are not fused with the carapace.

Ernst, Carl and Barbour,
    Roger, *Turtles of the United
    States,* 1972. University of
    Kentucky Press, Lexington.

Most clean, healthy turtles seem odorless to most humans; most, but not all. The classic examples of really odoriferous turtles are among the American musk and mud

17

Four North American turtles representing four genera of three different families: **Facing page:** *(top photo)* Chelydra serpentina rossignoni, *Chelydridae; (bottom photo)* Trionyx spinifer emoryi, *Trionychidae; (right)* Terrapene carolina mexicana, *Emydidae; and (below)* Pseudemys floridana hoyi, *Emydidae.*

turtles. This is the family Kinosternidae; some members of the family are equipped with glands located where the carapace and skin meet. When captured and until they become tame they will release their very distinctive musky odor at the slightest provocation. Some are called stinkpots, skillpots and stinking jims. Captive stinkpots when kept as pets do not cause any odor problems.

Vision
Turtles have sharp vision. They are also good at color discrimination. The Greek tortoise favors yellow flowers.

Intelligence
Turtles are not very bright. Most seem smarter than salamanders but not as smart as cats and dogs. They will learn to discriminate between some colors and some will even work their way through a simple maze, but a monkey would put all of turtledom to shame.

Sounds
Some large sea turtles and giant land tortoises are noisy, especially when they mate, but by and large most are mute. Noises come not only from their throats but also from the clicking of jaws and the rubbing of legs. Many sounds credited to turtles come from other sources and are reported inaccurately. For an exception to the rule, the big-headed turtle (*Platysternon*) actually screams when it is picked up.

Longevity
The records for longevity lend themselves to stretching. For example, there was and perhaps still is on the South Atlantic island of St. Helena a specimen which was reported to have been a pet of Napoleon during his imprisonment there. Later it was determined that Napoleon's turtle had died in 1877 and was replaced by the present claimant in 1882. This claimant's name is Jonathan. Another turtle on St. Helena fell over a cliff in 1918 and died at the age of 120 years plus whatever her age was at the time she arrived from Aldabra.

Another famous turtle was Tui Malila. Legends described it as a giant Galapagos land tortoise which was given by

Captain James Cook to the Queen of Tonga in 1773 or 1777. It finally expired on May 19, 1966. If no one played the shell game here, it represents the record for longevity. I advise you not to put any sincere money on a bet about it. Even though this narrative appears in several books, "it ain't necessarily so." Dr. Osmond P. Breland, while he was Professor of Zoology at the University of Texas, wrote that Captain Cook had

Seychelles tortoise which resided on the island of Mauritius for 152 years until it died in an accident in 1918. It seems that 1918 was a bad year for old turtles.

Ordinary American box turtles are believed to live for as long as 123 years, according to Archie Carr in

Stink-pot turtle, Sternotherus odoratus, *as its name indicates is a strong-smelling species. It is commonly distributed in the eastern areas of the United States.*

nothing to do with the transportation of *that* turtle, and furthermore, it wasn't even native to the Galapagos but rather to Madagascar.

I am convinced that Dr. Breland is right and the record of Tui Malila is not valid, but we do have an authentic record of a

his classic *Handbook of Turtles.* Also, Roger Conant tells us of an alligator snapping turtle that by 1948 had lived in the famous Philadelphia Zoo for 57 years. You might wish to find out whether it is still alive.

21

*Cryptodiran turtle species: (above)*Heosemys spinosa, *Southeast Asia; (below) Blanding's turtle,* Emydoidea blandingi, *United States;* **facing page:** *(top)* Graptemys kohni, *United States; (bottom)* Deirochelys reticularia chrysea, *United States.*

22

Introduction

Hibernation and Estivation

Reptiles that live in places where freezing occurs cope with this situation by hibernating. Their food supply is necessarily reduced, the ground and much of the water are impenetrable and since they have virtually no internal control of body heat they must lower their metabolic rate until living conditions improve. Some turtles hibernate under water in mud and some crawl into holes dug by other animals or by themselves; still others get themselves under mulch piles and into the earth. You can help to make the turtles' job easier by turning over the soil. The effect is the same. They sense that the days are growing shorter and the evenings are cooler and they begin to look downward for openings in the ground. A successful turtle in the frost belt will have grown quite fat over the summer, and it will live off this stored fat while it rests in a torpor until the balmy breezes blow again. Heartbeat and respiration will slow and energy requirements will drop off tremendously. Sometimes in springtime an early thaw will waken the turtles and bring them out too soon. Predators or a late frost will knock some off. This is nature's way, and there is not much you can do about it.

For captive turtles there is no hard and fast rule. My own experience has been that turtles kept inside should be kept awake 365 days a year. As the days grow shorter, you should provide extra warmth and longer daylight hours with artificial light. If a turtle is not fully hibernating, it may use up its stored fat and starve before it wakes enough to eat and assimilate the food it needs to keep going.

Garden turtles need only deep mulch piles and deep mud-bottom pools to do their thing naturally. How deep? Deep enough to get below the frostline. Obviously coastal Virginia doesn't have the depth of frost you will experience in Milton, Wisconsin or Alfred, New York or even mountainous Salem, West Virginia.

Estivation is another technique employed by turtles to cope with climate. Here the problem is drought and the process is to dig deep and lie quiet until more moisture becomes available.

Again, heartbeat and respiration slow down. Gopher tortoises in desert habitats may estivate several times in a year for a month or two if water or food is in short supply. Of course, this is something which will not happen to a cared-for captive.

offspring. To begin at a convenient landmark in anatomy, consider the reptilian heart. Most reptilian hearts have but three chambers, whereas mammals and birds possess four-chambered hearts. This means that there is some mixing of blood which was

Greek tortoise, Testudo hermanni, *is known to hibernate during the cold months of the year. It is a popular pet species in European countries, especially in Mediterranean countries.*

Metabolism

Most living things take in oxygen, water and food and then convert these things into movement, heat and

oxygenated in the lungs with blood which (although in circulation) did not pass through the lungs. This "imperfection" in the

Pleurodiran turtle species:
Facing page: *(top)* Pelusios gabonensis, *Africa; (bottom)* Phrynops rufipes, *South America;* **this page:** *(right)* Podocnemis expansa, *South America; and (below)* Phrynops nasuta wermuthi, *South America.*

27

circulatory system leaves the reptile with fewer heart parts to develop defects. Thus we call reptiles "cold-blooded." This "cold-bloodedness," like most things in nature, is a shade of gray and not absolutely cut and dried. For example, another reptile, the female python, does manage to heat her incubating eggs. As a matter of fact, the leatherback turtle has been proven to have internal temperature control.

This slow metabolic rate is an important fact of turtle life. They can go without food for long periods, especially if they are inactive, as during hibernation or estivation. They can go without breathing for long periods. A hibernating water turtle gets through the cold months of winter under water with a little trickery (see Respiration)

An active box turtle can close its shell for an hour or so with no apparent distress; it can also remain underwater for an hour without drowning if necessary.

When compared to a hummingbird with its tremendous appetite for nectar and its rapid wingbeat and its high body temperature, a turtle is way down at the other end of the metabolic scale.

Respiration

No turtle has gills. All turtles do have lungs. Trite, you say. Yes, but like so much in natural history, that's not the whole simple story. To begin with a more nearly whole story, a turtle in its bony shell cannot drive air in and out of its lungs with a conventional diaphragm, since such driving depends on the movement of a flexible rib cage. What turtles do (since their ribs are fused together to form the shell) is to pump air by movement of limbs and throat, and this movement alternately enlarges or reduces the lung cavity and thereby moves air. Also, it has been shown that as a turtle moves its head and neck in and out of its shell, a pumping action is accomplished. That's not all. Some water turtles have many tiny blood vessels close to the thin skin which lines the inside of the throat. More precisely, call it the pharyngeal cavity and liken it to their non-existent gills. A resting or hibernating turtle under water can obtain its necessary oxygen from that which is naturally dissolved in the water. This is accomplished by "breathing" water; call it pharyngeal respiration. And even that's not all! Some water turtles are also known to draw water through their anal openings into sacs associated with the cloaca where tiny capillaries and thin skin permit carbon dioxide to exit and oxygen to enter the bloodstream. And that's a fact.

A leopard tortoise, Geochelone pardalis, *found in southern and eastern Africa, as seen from the front. There is ample space between the carapace and plastron to permit some pumping action of the front limbs for respiration.*

Turtles show a wide range of structural and physiological differences: (left) the attractively marked head of Sacalia bealei, an emydid turtle from Asia; (below) note the strange head shape of Chelus fimbriata, the matamata, from South America; **facing page:** (top) fully adult female (larger specimen) and male Graptemys kohni, from the southern United States; (bottom) a good view of the alligator snapper, Macrochelys temmincki, from the United States.

Getting Started

This book was written for pet keepers and not for herpetologists. It is arranged so that the species are discussed in terms of habitat and not according to their systematic classification.

In no particular order, let's take a quick look at a few facts and a few precautions you should be aware of.

As I mentioned already, many turtle species are protected during certain seasons and/or in certain places. If you plan to collect your own specimens, know the law before you start out. You could be hauled into court and fined or even jailed for your ignorance.

The hours of daylight and/or the temperature might trigger a turtle to become lethargic in anticipation of wintertime hibernation. If your specimen is from an area where there are hard winters, you might have to provide artificial light and warmth to divert it from its natural inclinations.

Turtles in nature don't thrive in polluted waters. Some may survive, but this is not what pet keeping is all about. Don't crowd your animals. Start with one or two

in oversize accommodations and resist the temptation to possess one of each species. This pet-keeping hobby is not like stamp collecting. Once you take on an animal, you have taken on a responsibility. Fortunately, however, any turtle can get through a "long weekend" without you.

When you measure a turtle, consider only the straight line from the front to the back of the top shell. Don't measure over the curve if you want to have figures that are consistent with what you will find in the standard textbooks.

Always provide a shady place in your aquarium or terrarium or outdoor turtle pen. Turtles are "cold-blooded" animals, and since they cannot internally regulate their temperature, they must search out the degree of warmth that suits them.

Digestion of food is dependent not only on digestive juices but also on temperature. Your pet cannot do justice to a meal if, after it is fed, it is chilled. Death may result.

Since turtle eggs are

sometimes fertile (even after a couple of years since the last mating), it is a good idea to bury any that you may find and wait out three months—you may get a turtle or two this way.

So much for the loose ends. Now let's get down to the useful details.

HEALTH OF THE TURTLE YOU CHOOSE

You may purchase a specimen from a pet dealer or you may capture one; the source is not as important as the quality of the product. Don't start your hobby with a diseased animal or with a pig in a poke.

Examine the turtle carefully even if it will cost you nothing. It should be healthy, strong, plump and complete with two working eyes, a full set of claws and a normal-looking tail. Its shell should not be cracked. Some species do have one or two hinges on the bottom shell (plastron) and one genus (Kinixys) of Africa has a hinged top shell (carapace) but these hinges look like hinges and not like injuries.

Its eyes should be bright and clear regardless of their color. Colors range from yellow to red to brownish black, but there should never be a blue or milky cast to the eye of a healthy turtle.

The mouth and throat, if you are able to get a look, should be free of cheesy material or fungus. There should be no open sores. After you become adept at keeping turtles you may be willing to risk taking on a diseased individual because of its rarity and in the expectation that you can effect a cure, but don't start your hobby with less than a perfectly healthy animal.

If you spot a few ticks or leeches don't be concerned. Intoxicate them with a drop (or a wiping) of rubbing alcohol and then pick them off with a pair of tweezers.

A captive turtle too fat to pull fully into its shell is not necessarily ill, just fat. Check to be sure that it has strength in its limbs and then don't worry about the fat. A female about to lay a clutch of eggs will be hard put to withdraw fully into her shell, but again, this is not a disease.

Oversize or swollen eyes are a sure sign of trouble, generally incurable, frequently nutritional in origin. Turtles suffering from malnutrition and having "pop-eyes" are usually past saving.

Minor injuries will heal with no specific help from you. Give the animal clean quarters. Provide a place for sunning in direct unfiltered sunlight. Furnish a salt water bath for up to an hour of 3½% (seawater concentration) or a one-minute vinegar dip of 2½% (half-strength) daily to control infection. Try an Aureomycin, tetracycline or penicillin salve on minor infected wounds. Use a fungicide like Mycalog (Squibb) on fungus infections and, if you can afford it, by all means take an ill turtle to your veterinarian for specialized professional treatment.

If you discover roundworms in the feces of your pet, take it to the veterinarian for a treatment with Santonin or perhaps a piperazine formulation. You may be able to break the life cycle of these parasites by prompt removal of all fecal matter. Shell rot has reportedly been controlled by providing clean quarters, dry basking in sunlight and a careful clean-up of the

infected area followed by a treatment with tincture of iodine or tincture of gentian violet.

A naturally hard-shelled turtle with a soft shell is probably suffering from a calcium deficiency. It will need more calcium in its diet. *Whole* fresh fish served whole or in chunks or ground up will help if supplemented with vitamin D either as a diet supplement or in the form of

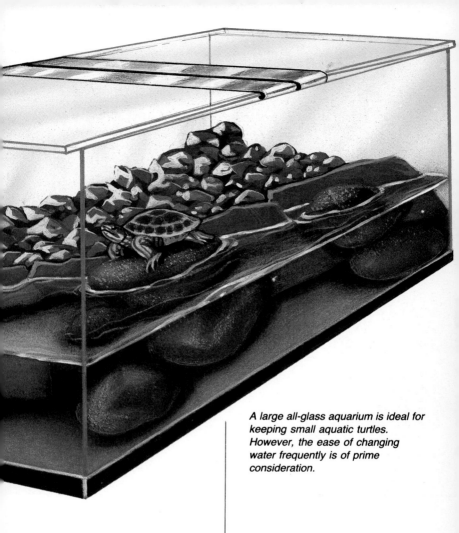

A large all-glass aquarium is ideal for keeping small aquatic turtles. However, the ease of changing water frequently is of prime consideration.

unfiltered sunlight. Bear in mind that most window glass filters out virtually all the ultraviolet rays with which the turtle is able to take advantage of the vitamin D in its diet.

COMPANIONS FOR TURTLES

A turtle may be kept with certain other animals in perfect harmony. There are very few rules and many combinations and some inconsistencies.

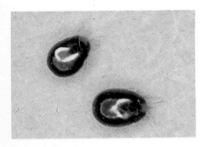

Ticks if present can be physically removed. Any tissue damage resulting from the removal of these parasites should be treated topically with antiseptics or antibiotics.

An attack of fungus can result in the loss of scutes, exposing the underlying bony parts of the carapace. The loss of scutes is permanent.

First the rules:

1.) Don't mix habitats. This makes for compromises, and no one gets a fair shake. An aquarium designed to accommodate a soft-shell (aquatic) and a gopher (terrestrial-desert) will accomplish neither job. The gopher will develop fungus and/or pneumonia from the excess moisture while the soft-shell will be lost to view in the mud.

2.) Give thought to predatory instincts. A snapper will eventually finish off any creature it can get hold of.

3.) Don't crowd. What you cannot accomplish in two square feet takes place in nature all the time on an acre (about 43,000 square feet).

Now, the combinations:

1.) Wood turtles and same-size frogs usually make it together.

2.) Box and Greek and gopher turtles are compatible.

3.) Diamondbacks get on nicely with each other, but they must have brackish water, and most other turtles belong in fresh water.

4.) Snakes and lizards do all right with all but snappers

and soft-shells, so long as the habitats are similar.

5.) Toads and terrestrial turtles are compatible.

6.) Crocodiles, alligators and caimans should *not* be kept with any turtles.

7.) A few fish in an aquatic habitat aquarium are O.K. Guppies can usually safely live in a tank with a common snapping turtle. It might just ignore them if it is well fed. A soft-shell will eat all aquarium fish with gusto.

8.) Waterspiders and water boatmen are O.K. with aquatic turtles, although some will get eaten. Leeches are dangerous parasites.

9.) Gopher turtles are sometimes found in the company of burrowing owls (yes, owls), but your chances of finding a pet dealer who stocks burrowing owls for gopher turtle cages are slim.

Now let's consider the inconsistencies. These usually relate to size or crowding or hunger. You must use your own powers of intelligence and observation. Don't mix diurnal and nocturnal animals; they will keep each other awake (most land turtles are diurnal, some aquatic turtles are not). Don't starve a snapper and expect

it to ignore a bullfrog, regardless of the sizes. Incidentally, a two-pound bullfrog can turn the tables and easily swallow a hatchling snapping turtle.

Another example of the inconsistencies takes place in tropical fish or goldfish

A stroll under the sunshine for your pet turtle is always beneficial. But, be sure that there is a shady area close by where it can seek refuge if the temperature gets too high.

aquariums into which a hatchling red-ear is introduced. Fish and turtle ignore each other until the turtle gets hungry or the fish get careless or too familiar. Usually you will be warned by signs of clipped fins before fatalities result. Remember that if you do put a red-ear in an aquarium with fish, you should provide a floating island since this species is not totally aquatic; it does want to dry out and bask from time to time.

A minor point about companions for predatory turtles is a matter of disparity

The lack of dentition in turtles is replaced by powerful beaks that are capable of tearing fibrous plant material. When maintained on soft foods for extended periods, turtles can develop overgrown beaks that will require trimming.

of size. To take an extreme case, place a nine-inch snapping turtle in an aquarium containing various sizes of one species of fish and take note of which (if any)

fish disappear. You will likely discover that your nine-inch snapper will totally ignore any fish less than one inch long. If the turtle is well fed it may ignore all the fish, but if it gets hungry it may begin to pick off the larger specimens. This probably will take place at night. Now, replace that nine-inch turtle with a hatchling and then the large fish will survive (perhaps with nipped fins), but the smaller individuals will begin to go. In other words, it is possible to keep prey and predator together if you do some thoughtful planning.

A woodland or desert habitat permits lizard/turtle combinations. Anoles, skinks and "horned toads" (which actually are lizards) have all been kept with land tortoises. These lizards are all predators upon insects, and the terrestrial turtles are scavengers and vegetarians, so there is no problem on that score. Small snakes may also be kept with land turtles if you observe precautions about escapes and use some judgment about sizes. If there is some doubt in your mind about cagemates, my advice is—don't try it.

Caymans (also spelled caimans) and other crocodilians should not be kept with any turtles. Bullfrogs and green frogs (genus *Rana*) should not be kept with aquatics or semi-aquatics. Invariably one or the other gets eaten. A frog will attempt prodigious feats of swallowing oversize objects and will frequently succeed or die trying. By way of contrast, toads do get along with terrestrial turtles; conveniently, they have no foods in common except perhaps earthworms.

For a beginning hobbyist with turtles, I suggest that your challenge should start with just one specimen, all by itself.

SUITABLE TURTLE SPECIES

There are only about 221 species of turtles worldwide, and pet keepers must immediately eliminate the six species of sea turtles and two dozen species and subspecies of giant Pacific and Indian Ocean island tortoises (which are very strictly protected) and also perhaps twenty additional smaller species worldwide

which are rare, endangered and hopefully protected. Next we should, as beginners, turn our backs on perhaps two dozen additional delicate and difficult species even if we

A typical setup for keeping pet turtles a few years ago. Such relatively small housing units for aquatic turtles have been replaced in many cases by fish tanks, which provide much more space and can be filtered and heated efficiently.

can afford the purchase price. It is absurd and needlessly cruel to possess an animal which is sure to fade away rapidly.

39

This leaves us with about 150 species worldwide, any of which will challenge, amuse, delight and educate. Well, let's back off a bit. I'm not sure that many pet keepers, excepting perhaps the most dedicated herpetologists, derive much delight from keeping soft-shelled turtles.

If you have a choice (rather than a specimen thrust upon you), choose deliberately. Land turtles need less care since their feces tend to dry up and the odors and risks of decay and disease associated with warm water are not present. Semi-aquatics are more active, and this is a strong plus factor for many people. Aquatics are for the most part mean and ugly, but if you like the most ugly and most spectacular, consider the mata-mata and also reconsider the long-snouted, sharp-beaked, soft-lipped soft-shells.

Following is a listing of turtle species suitable for keeping by the inexperienced turtle keeper.

The best *semi-aquatics* are the: European pond turtles; geographics (map turtles); Reeve's turtle; sliders; cooters; painted; Spanish terrapin; side-necks (some); Malayan box turtles; mud and musk.

The best *aquatic* turtle is the: common snapping.

The best *terrestrial* turtles are the: box; Greek; wood (which is the least terrestrial in this group).

Many other varieties make great pets too, but these are the ones which will give you the least trouble as you get started.

HOW TO OBTAIN A TURTLE
Buy your first specimen from a pet shop. Later, when you know more about what you are getting into, catch your own.

Any terrestrial turtle that can outrun a thirteen-year-old red-blooded, all-American kid deserves its freedom. Slower terrestrial turtles need only be discovered and picked up. Some will void their bladders at the moment of capture or a few moments later—so don't promptly pocket them.

Aquatics and semi-aquatics are trapped, netted or captured by stealth—and that's not easy. They may have poor hearing, but they can certainly sense your approach by feeling vibrations. Their vision is acute. Commercial fishermen catch them in their seines; so can you. Also, you can catch aquatics with a barbless hook baited with an earthworm. You will be surprised to find that many aquatic turtles are very fast in water *and* on land.

Traps are tricky. Many traps are regulated by law. They must include a portion exposed to the atmosphere or your captive might drown before you get around to checking the trap. The pharyngeal and cloacal respiration mentioned elsewhere is usually sufficient only for resting or hibernating individuals, and it is not standard equipment on every species that goes into the water.

A turtle trap looks like a minnow trap with a larger funnel. A double funnel and "parlor" design is also effective. If you need only one or two specimens you would be well advised to order them from a local pet dealer if he doesn't already have what you want. If you control a small pond with a spillway you can always drain the pond and make your selection. Just don't do it right before a drought.

Once you get started, by all means join a herpetological association; you then will have ample opportunities to exchange specimens with other hobbyists.

Do not patronize any dealer who does not transport live turtles in a humane fashion. Horror stories of the great number of turtles suffocated during transport are well-known.

Reproduction

THE SEXES

Male turtles have longer and thicker tails than females of the same species. Additionally, the male's anal opening is farther from the base of the tail. The male is able to wrap his tail around and under the edge of the female's carapace when they mate.

In some species of pond turtles, the male turtles have longer front claws than their mates. These claws on painted turtles help a male to excite a female before they mate.

Male turtles in some species have brighter colored eyes than do the females. For example, the box turtle male frequently has red eyes, but the female frequently has brown eyes. Among turtles with notched plastrons under the tail, the male would be expected to have the deeper notch. Female turtles are likely to have flat or convex (bulging) plastrons. This gives them more room for egg storage. Male turtles are more likely to have flat or concave (hollowed) plastrons. This makes it easier for a

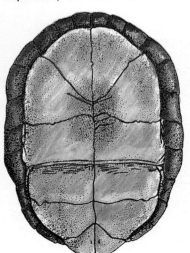

Plastron (concave or with a shallow depression) of a male turtle.

Plastron (flat or bulging) of a female turtle.

male to ride on a female's back during mating. It still really is not easy—they need all the help they can get.

In some species (soft-shells, for example) the female is larger. In some species (box turtles, for example) the male is larger.

cell has a male genetic complement (call it "y"), then the product of that union of sperm and ovum will result in a male offspring.

There are some notable exceptions. We know populations of certain

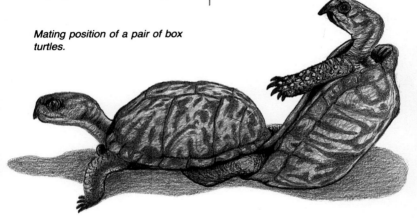

Mating position of a pair of box turtles.

If you wish to keep one pet turtle, its sex is unimportant. The diet and longevity and disposition of males and females are about the same.

The sex of most vertebrate animals is determined at that moment when the successful sperm cell and the available egg cell (ovum) unite. If this successful sperm cell has a genetic complement (call it "x") for the female gender, the union will produce a female offspring. If the sperm

species of lizards which are 100% female. Also, there are certain fishes which actually change their sex during the course of their lifetimes. Among turtles we now have a report that in some species each turtle gets its sex as a result of the incubation temperature *after* the eggs were laid. Two doctors at the University of Wisconsin recently reported in *Science* magazine that all of 562 map and painted turtles which hatched from eggs that were incubated at 77° F. were males. Also, they found that out of 531 hatchlings whose eggs had been incubated at 87° F., all but four turned out to be females. In another test (using soft-shelled turtles) these same researchers found that the incubation temperature did not influence the sex at all.

slightly prehensile to aid in making a connection, and some species are provided with a hooked scale on the male's tail to aid in keeping that vital connection.

A fertilized female may remain fertile for several years, but each successive clutch will contain fewer fertile eggs unless there is a re-mating.

Illustration of a turtle emerging from its leathery egg shell.

BREEDING

Turtles do not pair for life or even for a season. A male finds a female who acts or smells or looks "right" and he rubs her face with his long claws or butts her with the front of his shell or bites her legs, and eventually she may become receptive. If so, he climbs on her back and they copulate. His tail might be

Turtle eggs are always white, generally leathery, and often elliptical—but in some species they are spherical. The female lays them in a hole she dug by herself and later filled up again. The young of the smaller species generally hatch in two or three months; in northern climes an egg laid in September might not hatch until the following May. The eggs of the giant Pacific and Indian Ocean species hatch after six months. The size of a clutch runs from 200 to 300 for some sea turtles, about 80 for a large snapping turtle and perhaps five or six eggs for a painted turtle.

The hatchlings are active at birth. A hatchling cuts through its egg shell with a tiny egg tooth located on its nose. The egg tooth, having done its job, soon falls off. There is some scar tissue which also falls away from the plastron. This was the baby turtle's connection to its food supply in the egg. There is no parental care of the young by any species of turtle.

A previously fertilized female may lay eggs in captivity. If she buries them, you should leave them alone. If not, you might pack them loosely in slightly dampened sand or sphagnum moss. Store them in the dark at about 75° F.; if they are going to hatch, they will do so in two cr three months. Don't handle or turn them. The young will want to drink (but not necessarily eat) as soon as they dig out.

No one gets very far propagating pet turtles at home. There has been something of an industry in the lower Mississippi Valley raising red-ears and geographic turtles for the pet trade, but it is fraught with difficulties caused by legislation and regulatory agencies. This is a good business to keep out of.

Hatchlings of Greek tortoises, Testudo hermannii, *that were bred in captivity. If bred in winter, their holding cage will require heat.*

Feeding Your Turtle

Once upon a time the most readily available and inexpensive turtle in the U.S. pet trade was the red-ear, which were shipped everywhere as hatchlings even before their egg-sac scars were healed. The packaged food available for them then was dry ant pupae and/or dried ants. If that is all they got to eat, they would surely go blind from the formic acid in the ants' bodies or they would die of malnutrition. It was really sad.

Today turtles are much more expensive, "ant" food is no longer a favored product and more pet keepers and more pet dealers are better informed.

When we get to terrestrials, a box turtle loves a bit of chicken liver or hamburger now and then, but even a juvenile will do nicely on mushrooms, melon, beans, peas, grapes, bananas, leafy vegetables and water. It is really easy; just offer a variety and then watch carefully to see what they eat most avidly.

When in doubt, offer any turtle: earthworms, raw unfrozen fresh fish, snails, bananas, canned dog food, mushrooms, lettuce and pieces of melon. If it accepts none of these, it probably is sick or cold or terribly frightened. Remember, too, that aquatic and semi-aquatic species cannot eat unless they are under water.

Generally speaking, semi-aquatic turtles prefer to be eaters of fish, frogs, birds, carrion, worms, snails and crawfish. Freeze-dried tubifex worms available in your pet shop are an excellent protein food for semi-aquatics and aquatics. To a lesser extent water turtles will eat plants, especially if animal food is not available. As they grow

Turtles will not refuse any kind of snail offered. Some species of snails are inexpensive and available commercially.

older some species such as the red-ears and sliders will eat more plant life. By contrast, an aquatic soft-shell turtle is never much interested in plant life unless it is very hungry.

If you set up your aquarium for pond turtles you should bear in mind all the undigested food and feces and occasional eggs which may be laid and subsequently broken—all this material will become food for bacteria. The water color and odor will tell you what is happening, and this unpleasantness is really unnecessary.

turtles in a ten-gallon aquarium furnished with a minimum of gravel, five or six gallons of water, a sunning perch and sources of heat and light will go for months with just minimal maintenance and without the need for filtering the water. A couple of guppies or white-cloud mountain fish or perhaps a small goldfish could be added to pick up uneaten food scraps, and your turtles will thrive in crystal-clear water.

Now, double the number of turtles or halve the amount of water, or feed them more

Turtles that do well on diets providing a high percentage of meat can benefit from the meaty freeze-dried (and frozen) foods that are made for tropical fish; freeze-dried tubifex worms are especially relished.

For a few examples: Two three-inch painted or geographic or red-ear or spotted or musk or mud

heavily and chaos will surely result. Yes, you can crowd the animals or push the food but as you do, you must

You can give your pet turtle a few goldfish occasionally. The common goldfish is raised in large numbers and sold commercially for food of other fishes, birds and reptiles.

spend more time and effort cleaning up. You might try filtering the water—good! Plan to change the filter bed frequently; it will surely plug up. You may opt to completely change the water routinely. Good—this is also effective, especially if you feed your pets heavily.

How heavily? A pond turtle will eat a volume of food equal to half the size of its head every day. If you offer it twice as much, it probably will eat that too. If you provide it with only half as much it probably will survive, but will not likely grow and perhaps it will suffer from

nutritional diseases such as soft shell and blindness.

A four-pound gopher turtle might eat as much as a head of lettuce and a banana in one day. A two-pound snapper will pack away a quarter of a pound of fish daily.

Temperature has a lot to do with how much your pet will consume. Start at 75° F. (but never go above 95° F.) and then make adjustments as you continue to learn what suits your own specimen. Obviously, a tropical mata-mata wants more warmth than a New England stinkpot.

HOUSING TURTLES IN AQUARIA

For many situations, an aquarium turns out to be *the* enclosure for a pet turtle. It is easy to clean, water-tight, provides good viewing and is inexpensive. For many habitat arrangements it needs few or no modifications. Unfortunately, it is not ideal for all species unless it is modified, so let's look it over critically, considering the intended use.

The Desert Habitat: For gopher tortoises, Greek tortoises and their ilk you want the largest possible surface area covered with dry sand. Don't crowd the crawling area with gee-gaws and gimcracks. Also bear in mind that these species are powerful diggers, so anchor any rock or it will surely be undermined and could tip over to crush a specimen or break a side of the tank. If you must install a rock, glue it in place with silicone rubber aquarium cement available from your pet dealer. This product is excellent for permanently attaching glass, most minerals and some metals to glass, but it is worse than useless for wet wood.

The cover should not be glass, since the heat which desert species crave will cause high humidity and fungal diseases unless you

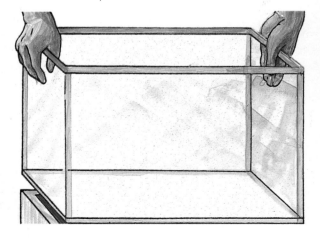

An all-glass aquarium permits viewing your pet turtle from all sides. Get the shape and size required by the type of turtle you intend to keep.

provide ample ventilation. For this situation, a quarter- or half-inch wire mesh makes a good cover. A light source is great for heat as well as illumination. Carefully choose the wattage to provide warmth but not cooking. Make sure that the desert habitat includes a shady area and a supply of clean drinking water. This will require some ingenuity on your part.

The required temperature for desert species may be achieved with electrical pads, but you must choose one which does not put out high temperatures, or cracked glass due to thermal shock (differential thermal expansion) will result. A heating pad which is never warmer than 90° F. on the surface is safe for this application. Pet shops sometimes carry these products for warming dog houses. Don't put the pad *in* the aquarium; instead mount the aquarium *over* the pad. Remember that after a few years or less on a varnished wooden table, a heating pad will have left its mark.

One way to economize with the space in an aquarium for a desert habitat is to create a shelf which is also a sunshade. Remember that

For housing strictly terrestrial turtle species, a small dish of water will be sufficient. The wire mesh cover provides ventilation and protection from would be intruders, your house pets perhaps?

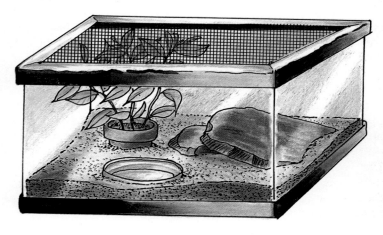

Shallow sided cages are not recommended for keeping terrestrial turtles. These turtles will certainly climb on the rock or each other and fall outside the cage from a considerable height and possibly break their shells and legs.

you must measure from the top of the shelf to the rim of the aquarium to assure that the largest turtle cannot reach the cover.

The shelf can be a piece of slate or a piece of wood cut to a loose fit and supported from the sides or the bottom or top edge of the tank. The support may be on brackets, legs or hangers—the choice is up to you.

The Woodland Pond Habitat: The water may be dished or the aquarium itself may hold the water. The former makes cleaning much simpler but the latter makes a more natural looking arrangement. This is like neckties—you pays your money and you takes your choice. Try to avoid mud-bottomed ponds in aquariums—they may look "natural," but after food and feces begin to decay you surely will not enjoy the odor of these naturally decomposing materials.

The cover should keep vermin and other pests out and your captives in. This is really not easy and it deserves your careful thought. Consider hinges, latches and heavy framing. Yelling at the dog will get you nowhere.

This flat piece of wood serves as a raft or platform for these red-eared turtles, Pseudemys scripta elegans. *Attempting to enhance the appearance of a turtle by painting the carapace is not recommended.*

The Aquatic Habitat: Many soft-shelled turtles will never leave the water except to lay eggs; some, however, will climb onto a shore or a floating log or stump to sun themselves. The same obtains for some mud and musk turtles and for snapping turtles and for the South American mata-mata.

Provide as much water as you can afford—large aquariums do get expensive. If you have a choice of shapes, try to get one that provides more surface area rather than great water depth. Water depth need be no greater than carapace length. The area should be at least three times as long and twice as wide as the length of the carapace. By this formula an eight-inch soft-shell should be in an aquarium with a minimum of 24 inches and a width of 16 inches. This is not a standard size in the aquarium trade, so you might have to settle for a tank 12 x 12 x 30 inches. This will have a nominal capacity of 20 gallons (actually more like 18.7 gallons) if filled and two-thirds of that (12.5 gallons) if filled to a depth of eight inches. The water will weigh $8\frac{1}{3}$ pounds per gallon and the tank will weigh perhaps twenty pounds additional. It needs a good substantial stand.

OUTDOOR HOUSING

Many turtle hobbyists have developed techniques for keeping their pets out-of-doors. Some do it in summertime only and others do it year-round. A Miami garden with protection against escapes and intruders will support any number of specimens and species—and most will never cease to be active except on the coldest days.

In Old Lyme, Connecticut, a terrestrial turtle out-of-doors will be active from June through September and intermittently in late spring and early autumn. Aquatic turtles enjoy the tempering effect of the water if it is sufficiently deep, and they will be active for all but the four coldest months of the year. In nature, some water turtles will be seen moving in water under ice. Therefore you may opt to keep your pet as a captive indoors or as a semi-captive indoors or outdoors or back and forth. Here are a few suggestions.

The enclosure should enclose not only above-ground but also underground. A *minimum* depth of two feet is important to keep predators out and pets in.

The fencing material and height are also important. Stinkpots do climb! An overhang may help to keep your pets inside.

If there is a frost where you live, you must provide for it.

A setup for aquatic turtles. It includes a ramp for reaching a platform outside the water, a drain for removing water, and an overhead lamp that gives light and heat.

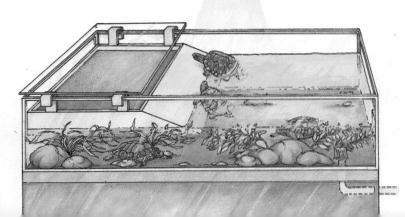

Your pet must be able to bury itself below the frostline. A pit heaping full of leaf and grass clipping mulch is a good hibernation site. You provide the site and your pet will likely bury itself there when the days grow shorter. Don't tamper with natural arrangements. The system is in delicate balance. A hibernating turtle, if too cold, will freeze and die. A hibernating turtle if too warm will remain slightly active and will beat more heartbeats, breathe more breaths, burn more energy and use up more stored energy supplies of glycogen and fat, thus exhausting its reserve before it is warm enough in springtime to eat and digest its food. It may then starve to death. Make up your mind and be consistent.

If you want your pet to be an outside pet, good. Provide it with a well drained, well insulated, deep hibernation site and leave it strictly alone.

If you want your pet to be an inside pet, give it warmth and full-length daylight hours with artificial light right through the winter.

Some keepers of native turtles provide food and water in an unfenced garden, and their charges never leave even though they are not fenced or tethered. This scheme works fine so long as there are no predators and few automobiles in the area.

If you want your pet indoors in winter and outdoors in summer, this too will work.

ESCAPES

This section is not intended to be an "I told you so," but frequently it works out that way, so I might as well keep it brief.

Captive turtles have little else to do except dream of roaming. No matter how much love, affection, sunlight, earthworms and melons you may lavish on them, there is still that dream of the open road in every turtle's mind. Obviously, they really don't know what's good for them.

A cage is only as high as its shortest vertical distance. This sounds trite, but you should bear in mind that three inches of gravel makes a 12-inch-high tank into a nine-inch-high tank, and if there is a rock or a piece of wood on the gravel, you must measure from the top of that point.

AQUATIC TURTLES
Soft-Shelled Turtles

Here in my study as I write is a Chinese soft-shelled turtle. I acquired it in Taiwan during a 1966 visit made for the publisher of this book. It was then a hatchling, hardly larger than a silver dollar. Today its shell is about seven inches long and the specimen probably weighs somewhat over a pound. It is either *Trionyx sinensis* or *Trionyx steindachneri*; I never tried to find out which.

This turtle is housed in a ten-gallon aquarium furnished with a 20-watt strip heater *on the outside.* Any interior equipment would surely be destroyed by this strong, active and undisciplined animal. About three pounds of gravel plus five inches of water comprise the entire habitat. It needs no rocks, no plants, no ramp for it to crawl out of the water. Just a little gravel and water and an outside heater. This turtle eats earthworms, lean beef, fish fillets, shrimp, live fish, crayfish, crabs, dog food, beef and chicken liver and more of the same at any time. If I let it eat its fill, it

Florida soft-shell, Trionyx ferox, *is the largest trionychid of the New World. It can measure as much as 18 inches in total length. It is trapped mostly for food.*

would probably never stop eating. I have fed it as much as a quarter pound of meat and fish daily and it showed no signs of being satisfied.

The ten-gallon tank, the base of which measures only 10 by 20 inches, is really much too small. This reptile should be in a 12 x 36 aquarium. The larger the aquarium and the more you feed an animal like this, the more frequently you will have to change the water. Don't filter it. *Change* it. Any filter on the market will be broken or upset by this powerful beastie. Further, the solid wastes generated will require a filter bed of perhaps ten cubic feet to handle the wastes from one specimen if you push the food. Pet keepers' aquarium filters do have a place in some aquatic or semi-aquatic turtle arrangements, but for a large soft-shell or a large snapper, these systems are out of the question. In public aquariums and zoos, when filter systems are used they occupy more space than do the exhibits, and they are provided with heavy-duty stainless steel drains.

For about seven years this soft-shelled turtle was kept with a Florida mud turtle and the two ignored each other. The mud turtle did climb out of the water onto a ramp every day for a few hours, but the soft-shell was never anything but fully immersed except to breathe.

It ate under water, slept under water, it hunted for fish and worms under water, defecated under water. In its natural state the female would leave the water only to lay her eggs. Soft-shell turtles even mate under water. Some are reported to float on the surface or to crawl onto a muddy shore to bask in sunlight, but this Chinese specimen of mine never showed any interest in sunbathing.

This turtle should ideally be kept alone. Since it is a great scratcher and scraper it will surely injure another soft-shell, and in a small tank with high concentrations of bacteria the risk of infection is dangerously high. Handle soft-shells with great care. They scratch and bite without provocation.

The best way to care for any species of soft-shell is to keep no more than two, and preferably just one, individuals in an aquarium

A specimen of Trionyx *photographed in a public aquarium.*

with no other companions. The tank bottom should be bare or covered with coarse gravel. Be prepared to drain the tank once weekly or more frequently if you feed it heavily. No plants, no rocks, no decorations, no gadgets. A piece of driftwood for a perch is the limit for "furniture." You really have to like a soft-shell to be willing to care for one.

As to temperature, no species of soft-shell needs more than an average of 80° F., but at temperatures less than 68° F. a tropical form may begin to get sluggish. If you are doubtful, start at 72° average temperature. Evenings could bring it down to 65° and daytimes the reading might go up to 82° for a perfect set-up. To achieve these temperatures, you should have the tank in a heated room or on a thermostatically controlled heat pad or another *external* heat source.

The tank should be deeper than the full length of the animal from its extended snout to an extended hind leg. Less depth will invite an escape. A glass tank cover which is at less than that height will surely be upset, and on falling you risk a big puddle on the floor and a cooked or electrocuted specimen.

Some filters designed for use with fish aquariums are excellent to use in setups housing aquatic and semi-aquatiac turtles. The aquarium filters known as "power" filters, for example, are very efficient at filtering and recirculating the water. Many such filters can operate even if the depth of the water in the tank is low, so they're excellent for use in turtle tanks that are only partially filled.

A soft-shell is not an ideal turtle for a beginner. The seven or so soft-shell genera are included in the family Trionychidae (sometimes known as Cyclanorbidae). Here is a list of the generic names you will encounter:

Lissemys (also called *Amyda*) India and Ceylon, to 8", one species

Chitra Southern Asia, to 3 feet, one species

Dogania (also called *Trionyx*) Southern Asia, to 10", one species

Cyclanorbis African, to 20", two species

Cycloderma African, to 15", two species

Pelochelys S.E. Asia, over 4 feet, one species

Trionyx (also called *Amyda*) Four species in North America

and one species in Africa and ten species in Asia

This adds up to 23 species, but some experts rank certain subspecies as species, so they count 27 species. In each of the above, the females tend to be larger than the males.

The largest American form is the Florida soft-shell, *Trionyx ferox.* This species grows to 18″ carapace length; it lives in lakes, ponds and canals.

The most commonly encountered U.S. species is *Trionyx spinifer.* It is commonly called the spiny soft-shell. Several subspecies are recognized. These various spiny soft-shells might grow to 17 inches carapace length for a female and only one-half that for a male.

In the U.S. another common species is the smooth soft-shell, *Trionyx muticus.* Females grow to 14 inches and, again, males are but half that size. They bite and scratch effectively, but at least their "shells" do not rasp.

Wild soft-shelled turtles eat waterfowl (young ducks mostly), crayfish, fish, frogs, crickets, grasshoppers, earthworms, snails and mussels.

Snapping Turtles
There are two U.S. species of snapping turtles. The alligator snapping turtle is found from central Illinois south to the Gulf of Mexico, west well into Texas and east through central Alabama and south Georgia and north Florida. Call it *Macroclemys temmincki* and confuse it only with the common snapping turtle, *Chelydra serpentina.* This common snapper is common indeed. It is found in relative abundance in every state from the Great Plains eastward. If you look down on a common snapping turtle, its eyes don't show. Both species are tough and ugly. They will eat anything that is digestible or even slightly digestible.

The alligator snapper has a wormlike lure in its mouth which it uses to attract fish to

Foods specifically compounded for consumption by turtles are available at pet shops in a number of different forms.

their death. In contrast to the common snapper, it is not likely to be found in brackish water. The alligator snapper is one of the world's largest turtles, excepting only the sea turtles. Records of specimens weighing 219 pounds have been authenticated, and a 403-pounder has been reported.

The common snapper is smaller, equally ugly, equally voracious, long-lived, tough, pugnacious and easy to keep in an aquarium. Fifty pounds is not quite the top weight, but a thirty-pounder will satisfy anyone I know for any purpose I know.

Regarding their toughness, I have seen common snappers crawling in the mud under ice, and a snapping turtle heart will pump vigorously for hours after it has been dissected from its beheaded owner. Snappers eat fish, carrion, small turtles, snakes, muskrats, frogs, invertebrates and plants. If a duckling swims close they will nip off a leg or if possible consume it entirely. My five-pounder eats road-killed sparrow-size birds—whole. Incidentally, even most road-killed birds are protected (although they are dead) by

the federal migratory bird act. Watch out! There may be a watch-bird watching you.

Don't lodge any snapping turtle in a small aquarium with *any other* creature, regardless of disparity in size. They don't get along even with their *own kind*, even while they are mating. I have kept a few snapping turtles captive in the course of the past fifty years, and here are my accumulated observations. First, I've never known one to become "tame." They will be shy but mean when first caught and after a year or two they will lose their shyness and become bold but will still be mean.

Young captive snappers will eat worms, fish, beef, liver, snails, clams, tadpoles, crayfish, crickets, grasshoppers and dog food. They will eat only under water. Large snappers will eat more of the same in the same way. I have fed a ten-inch (carapace length) snapper a quarter-pound of cut-up raw fish, and thirty minutes later it was ready to repeat the performance. Large captive snappers will eat mice, road-killed birds, kibbled dog food and—when they are hungry—vegetable matter. It may surprise you to open the stomach of a large wild snapper (over ten pounds) and find it full of cut-up plants. I believe this happens when in a pond or stream there are just too many turtles and not enough animal food.

Large snappers will eat frogs. They will also eat small turtles of all species. The only foods that don't seem to be completely assimilated are animal fats.

I have never handled a snapper that weighed over thirty pounds although I know that they do grow to fifty pounds. One thing I am sure of is that no thirty-pound snapper I've ever seen is capable of biting off the end of a broom handle. I have no doubt that a thirty pounder could easily remove a person's finger, but to cut through a one-inch thick broomstick, never. I doubt that even a fifty-pound snapper could get through a wooden broomstick.

Snapping turtles will tolerate badly polluted water, but that they like it is another matter. In nature, they are found in clean water. They will survive

A snapping turtle can be held by the tail for purposes of lifting it. However, it can be damaged extensively if it is held by the tail over a long period of time.

temperatures as high as 90° F. for short periods. They will thrive in water which is quite salty, up to 20% of seawater saltiness for extended periods and up to 50% for shorter periods. In fact they will probably get rid of their external parasites (such as leeches) this way.

Snappers will survive drought and mild frost and starvation for long periods with no apparent lasting damage.

61

You can easily kill a snapper by cutting off its head or by placing it in a freezer for a couple of weeks. If a large snapper or any other large turtle is carried by its tail, irreparable damage leading to eventual death may result.

The scales on a snapper shell don't flake off or molt but simply grow as the turtle grows.

One captive snapper was kept in an undersize aquarium and managed to get trapped on its back so that it could not right itself or reach the surface to breathe. Four days later it was assumed dead, but in fact that turtle is still alive and well to this day. We can assume that pharyngeal and cloacal breathing took over and carried it through.

So much for aquatic turtles. Now let's consider the more popular and desirable semi-aquatics.

SEMI-AQUATIC TURTLES

Look for sliders, red-ears, painteds, geographics, chicken turtles, diamondbacks, mud, musk and spotted species. Some will be available from time to time in your pet shop and still others are usually captured in ponds or purchased from twelve-year-old boys. All the semi-aquatics eat under water and may be fed any raw or live animal so long as it is low in fat or fat-free. You will discover that most turtles don't digest fatty foods. Try freeze-dried tubifex worms, crickets, fish, liver, earthworms, lean beef and dog food. Some species of semi-aquatics will do best on animal foods while they are young but can (and will) eat vegetable matter as they grow older. Offer them lettuce and if they eat it you can branch out to exotic foods such as spinach souffle. Really!

Elsewhere I mentioned a heat tape or a heating pad for warming a turtle tank. Small aquatic turtles will do nicely in an aquarium with a conventional aquarium heater. An overhead light is another good way to heat an aquarium housing semi-aquatic or terrestrial turtles. Always remember, though, that a shady area should be provided so that you don't cook your pets if the light should prove too hot.

All turtles need sunlight, and you should not deprive them of it. Again, as with aquatics, an aquarium should be your base of operations. The bigger the better; your pets will grow and invariably you will obtain new specimens as time goes on.

Don't slope gravel. For one thing, your pets will soon unslope it. For another thing, you will need too much gravel to provide water depth and dry area. Instead, design a wood board or driftwood arrangement which will provide the maximum water space and still offer a ramp with a dry area. Your semi-aquatic turtle will eat under water, so it doesn't really need a marching field, just a sunning perch out of water. The less "furniture" you pack into the aquarium, the easier it will be to keep it clean. If you find that you must keep your turtles in water which is full of uneaten food and fecal matter because the cleaning is such a chore, then you have no business keeping turtles. Gravel is hard to flush, siphon and otherwise keep clean, but a piece of

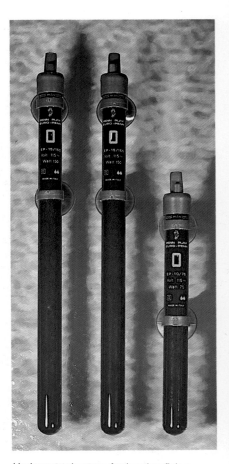

Underwater heaters for heating fish tanks can be utilized in providing heat to an aquatic turtle tank, too. For terrestrial turtles, undertank heating pads or dry heaters are used.

driftwood is easy to drain and rinse.

Remember that your turtle will not stop climbing when it reaches the highest point inside the tank. Be sure that no part of the driftwood or ramp is within a turtle-length of the rim. If you have "furniture" in an aquarium and a specimen is missing, don't accuse anyone of stealing it until you look behind the radiator. If you have a cat, cover the cage with a framed screen.

Mud And Musk Turtles

In the semi-aquatic family Kinosternidae, we have the musk and mud turtles. These little fellows make good pets. Some are sometimes slightly smelly until they become tame. They are hardy, long-lived and easy to feed. These turtles are not colorful, ranging from mud gray to mud black. In some species old males develop tremendous heads.

The family Kinosternidae includes two American genera, *Sternotherus* (the musk turtles) and *Kinosternon* (the mud turtles). Their habits and general appearance and requirements in captivity are

all the same. The largest mud or musk turtle carapace will caliper less than six inches. Various species and subspecies are found over most of the U.S., southern Canada and northern Mexico, except in four or five westernmost states.

Mud and musk turtles love to bask in branches of trees overhanging slow meandering streams and ponds. A mud turtle really does look ludicrous in the branches of a tree. When frightened, they drop into the water and swim into the mud. I'm reminded of the bald-headed man in the open convertible who tried to sue the state of New York because a protected sea gull dropped a clam on his head as it attempted to crack the shell. The man did not collect; the courts said it was an "Act of God."

Your musk or mud turtle will enjoy a basking perch, but it might well spend most of its time in water. It will surely eat under water, and several species are also reported to eat on land as well. Feed them on meat and fish (preferably small whole fish so they can benefit from the calcium in the fish bones).

They will also eat crustaceans, insects, snails, mussels, worms and small quantities of succulent vegetation.

pet keepers according to habitat preference rather than systematic classification. As you read this book, consider a semi-

When viewed from the plastral surface, the reduced condition of the plastron of a stink-pot, Sternotherus odoratus, *is very evident. The soft areas between the scutes are wider, too.*

Emydid Turtles

The family Emydidae is a large group which includes many American freshwater and marsh turtles (as well as the box turtles, which are primarily terrestrial). Let's look at the semi-aquatics of this family here, remembering that this book is organized for

aquatic as a turtle that spends as much time on land as in the water, and try to provide housing to match. It's really not too easy if you have less than three square feet to work with.

The spotted turtle, *Clemmys guttata,* is a good example of a semi-aquatic.

Above: marine turtles, like this loggerhead turtle, Caretta caretta, *have to be kept in an aquatic environment of great proportions such as an oceanarium. Keeping marine turtles in captivity, except under special conditions, is also not legal.* **Facing page:** *soft-shell turtles, (top)* Trionyx spinifer asper, *from the southern United States and a very large soft-shell from Southeast Asia, (below)* Chitra indica, *also require an aquatic environment.*

You will find it in pet shops and on reptile dealers' lists and wild all over southern New England. It also ranges south through southern New York, Pennsylvania, New Jersey, Maryland, Delaware and the coastal plain south to northern Georgia. From Pennsylvania it also ranges west into Michigan and Indiana. It grows to five inches and has a hard shell and no hinges. The carapace is smooth and black with small yellow spots scattered about. Conant tells us that in Ohio he found specimens

with as few as 14 and as many as 114 spots.

The plastron is yellow with black blotches. This species makes a fine pet. The female lays but three or four eggs which in Connecticut are usually buried in June and hatch in September.

This inoffensive little turtle is not protected in most of its range. It is hardy and attractive. It eats insects, earthworms, carrion and little or no vegetation. Captive specimens eat dog food too. It is closely related to the less aquatic wood turtle.

Also in this family is the European pond turtle, *Emys orbicularis.* This species is a popular European pet. It is long-lived and easy to maintain in a large aquarium.

The red-ear is the American turtle which has been kept by more people than any other species; perhaps more than all other species combined. For many years it was *the* five-and-ten-cent-store pet department *piece-de-resistance.*

Scientifically, it is *Pseudemys* (or *Chrysemys*) *scripta elegans.* The British know it as the elegant terrapin. It is but one subspecies of a half-dozen found in the Mississippi Valley, Gulf Coast and southeastern states, but excluding southern Florida. Baja California and western Mexico also have recognized subspecies. Since the red-ear is (and has been for many years) the turtle of small boys, it may show up anywhere out of its normal range; don't be surprised. Also, don't be too anxious to positively identify the subspecies you possess. This will get you nowhere. The various subspecies' habits are similar and they do intergrade. Some herpetologists even suggest rearranging the entire genus, then all your effort would be like wine down a rat hole. The key to the genus as proposed by Carr runs on for over four pages. Additionally, old males sometimes become black (melanistic) and there are otherwise responsible people who have tried to grant these individuals a separate position in the Tree of Life. This would be much akin to picking bald-headed men (like me) out of *Homo sapiens.* No way! Suffice it to say that these turtles have webbed feet, they lack plastron hinges, most are conspicuously marked with yellow and green, the males have long claws and all make good pets.

Here are the names of some of the more "prominent" North American mainland subspecies in case you are curious:

Pseudemys scripta

The long claws on the forelimbs of this illustration of a river cooter *Pseudemys concinna* indicate its sex as a male. The long claws provide a strong grip of the female during mating.

elegans — Red-eared turtle

P.s. scripta — Yellow-bellied turtle

P.s. troosti — Cumberland turtle

P.s. gaigae — Rio Grande turtle

P.s. nebulosa — from Baja California

Semi-aquatic turtles include the relatively drab American mud turtles, (above) Ki-nosternon *species; (below)* Sternotherus minor minor *and* **facing page:** *some of the more attractively colored and patterned Asiatic (top),* Geoclemys hamiltoni, *and (bottom) European emydid species,* Emys orbicularis.

P.s. hiltoni — from western Mexico (Sonora)

P.s. taylori — from Coahuila, Mexico

For pet keeping purposes I suggest that you lump all the *Pseudemys scripta* subspecies and all the closely related *P. rubriventris* into one section. As one might suspect, the number one example of *P. rubriventris* is the red-bellied turtle, *P.r. rubriventris.* It is found from New Jersey to North Carolina on the coastal plain; the largest confirmed size is 15 inches, but 18 inches has been reported. A small pocket of *P. rubriventris bangsi* is native to Plymouth County, Massachusetts. The differences between it and other subspecies are very technical and of interest only to herpetologists.

Still one more turtle in this series of water-loving semi-aquatics is *P. nelsoni,* the Florida red-bellied turtle. Males grow to eleven inches and females to thirteen inches.

Now, to wind it up for *Pseudemys,* there is the *floridana* section of "cooter" turtles, difficult to identify, easy to keep and delicious to eat. I might mention here that virtually every turtle has been eaten somewhere by someone. Certain species are more desirable, but unless one spends a lifetime in gastronomic research, most stewed turtle meat tastes about the same. This *floridana* section of *Pseudemys* includes eight subspecies or races from Virginia south to Florida and west into Texas and Oklahoma.

Many *Pseudemys* turtles are found near saline tidal marshes, and frequently a red-ear or one of its near relatives will be found swimming in brackish water. This is good to remember if you have a specimen that is infested with leeches or suffers from skin infection. Give it a daily dip in natural or artificial seawater.

Most are omnivorous as juveniles and as they grow older they tend to consume proportionally more vegetable matter. All eat under water and a few may also eat on land. When in doubt, start out with offers of fresh raw fish, earthworms, chicken liver, melon and lettuce.

In the great family Emydidae, the genus

Chrysemys provides pet keepers with a few gems which are hard to tell from *Pseudemys.* Don't try too hard; call them painted turtles and find them over southern Canada and 75% of the U.S. from Washington to Maine.

Their distribution skips all of Florida and virtually all of Texas. There are none in California, Nevada and Utah. All of the other lower 48 have some *Chrysemys picta* subspecies. This is a hard-shelled turtle with no hinges, no sculpturing and no sawtooth edges on the carapace. The tail is slender. The feet are webbed for swimming, and the male grows long claws which he uses to caress his intended mate. The plastron is colored plain yellow or yellow with irregular black blotches. The top of the carapace is the color of a ripe black olive. The distinctive marking are on the *margin* of the top and the *underside* of the carapace. Red bands and bars are attractively arranged here on painted turtles. They look painted on, but be assured they are perfectly natural. The carapace of a large painted turtle might measure seven inches.

Illustration of the very well-known red-eared turtle, Pseudemys scripta elegans *showing the characteristic marking on the side of the head.*

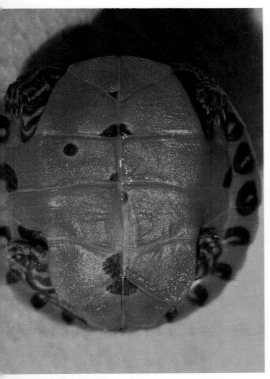

Native American emydid turtles are among the most available species for keeping in a semi-aquatic environment: (left) plastral view of the aptly named red-bellied turtle Pseudemys nelsoni; (below) southern painted turtle, Chrysemys picta dorsalis; **facing page:** (top) spotted turtle, Clemmys guttata; and (bottom) diamondback terrapin, Malaclemys terrapin, the subspecies M. t. macrospilota is seen here.

There was a time when some people thought it was "cute" to paint "decorations" on living turtles. The paint was so tough and tenacious that to remove it was to kill the turtle—but to let it remain was equally cruel, since it inhibited normal shell growth. This practice is a dead issue now, but it is mentioned here simply to make it clear that the common name for *Chrysemys picta* has absolutely nothing to do with this artificial decoration.

Painted turtles will do just fine in aquariums furnished with basking racks or shelves. They will usually eat under water, and you will find that they prefer animal food.

Cuttlefish bone is a good source of calcium for your pet turtle. It can be pulverized and mixed with the food.

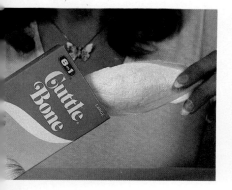

Earthworms, tadpoles, small fish or large fish cut up, crickets, grasshoppers, crayfish, mussels, clams, snails and chicken livers are all good fare. Assure good nutrition by offering variety. Remember that all turtles must have calcium for bone growth and that the best source of calcium for carnivorous animals is animal bone. The other necessary ingredient is vitamin D, which is necessary in order to facilitate the absorption of the calcium. You can supply vitamin D in diet supplements available from your pet dealer and you can arrange for your pets to get direct sunlight— not filtered through glass, since most glass will stop most ultra-violet "U.V." rays.

Terrapins

Now, let's consider the fabled diamondback terrapins of the genus *Malaclemys*. There is but one species, *Malaclemys terrapin*, and seven subspecies or races. Diamondbacks are found from the Texas Gulf Coast all the way around Florida and north to Cape Cod.

All are beautiful turtles with spotted or blotched heads, necks and legs. The base skin color is a pale gray, and the markings are dark gray or black. The carapace shield is sculptured in an attractive pattern, but not as deeply as with a wood turtle. The plastron is not hinged. The feet are webbed. The animal is elusive in the tidemarshes; many visitors to marshes never see one, although their boats might be plowing through waters full of them.

were depleted. This was done to satisfy the marketplace. Today the demand is down and wild specimens suffice. The owner of a nine-inch carapace would be a whopper and would surely be a female. Six inches is about right for an adult male.

The diamondback terrapin, Malaclemys terrapin, *is truly a colorful and beautifully patterned turtle. It is a well-known and extensively studied American turtle species.*

For starters, don't try to find out which race or subspecies you are looking at; they intergrade, and further they have been deliberately crossed by people who developed techniques for propagating them commercially during the period when their numbers

This species has been studied more intensively than any other American turtle because of its popularity as a gourmet food. The U.S. Bureau of Fisheries operated a station at Beaufort, N.C. for almost 40 years and published a tremendous amount of its findings over

The genus Pseudemys *has a wide range over North and South America and includes a number of species that can be kept in a semi-aquatic habitat:* **facing page:** *(top) young* Pseudemys scripta dorbigny, *from Brazil; (bottom)* Pseudemys decorata, *from Haiti;* **this page:** *(right)* Pseudemys concinna, *from the southern United States; and (below)* Pseudemys scripta venusta, *from Mexico.*

the years.

The first two points you must remember about these handsome animals is that they are never found far from water and they are never found in fresh water. You must be able to taste saltiness of the water you put into the aquarium if you expect to keep this species.

The saltiness or brackishness of a tidal creek or estuary is extremely variable, but the diamondback turtle thrives in it. One possible advantage to this turtle is that variable salinity will work against the turtle's parasites—leeches, for example, are not found in brackish waters. How salty is brackish? Well, as the tides and winds and run-off vary, so the salinity varies. Sea water is about 3½% salt by weight. This figure is usually expressed as 3.5% or 35ppt (parts per thousand). Salt, sodium chloride (NaCl)—the same as what we sprinkle on our food—is the major constituent, but traces of virtually all the elements on earth are also found in the sea. The best way to provide your *Pseudemys* or snapper or diamondback with brackish water is to purchase

sea water salts from your pet dealer and make up a solution of one-third to one-half strength—that is, mix into the water just ⅓ to ½ of the amount of salt recommended for a marine aquarium.

A gallon of water weighs about eight pounds or 128 ounces. For ⅓ of sea water salinity we would need ⅓ x 3.5% x 128 ounces of salt for every gallon of water. Multiplication of 0.33 x .035 x 128 equals 1.478 ounces of salt by weight. If you don't have a sensitive balance, ask your friendly pharmacist or postmaster to help you. Don't worry about that third decimal—remember that anything from ⅓ to ½ salinity would be O.K.

Table salt usually has an additive to keep it free-flowing and this additive may cloud the water in your terrarium or aquarium. Cooking or coarse Kosher salt does not necessarily contain the trace elements found in seawater, so if you want to properly dot the i's and cross the t's use sea water salt—your pet shop surely stocks it.

Diamondbacks will spend 90% of their time under

water. Provide a basking shelf or a large float, and the remainder of their home should be clean brackish water. A gravel bottom is O.K. so long as you can siphon up the debris. Filter tubing will be upset unless it is heavy stainless piping installed by a plumber or a steamfitter. You might find it convenient to make up enough salty water for several siphonings and store it in gallon plastic milk jugs. Another option would be to make up a concentrated brine solution and calculate the number of ounces per gallon of tap water necessary to bring the contents of the tank to river mouth or tidemarsh brackishness.

Diamondbacks eat mollusks such as mussels, snails, young oysters and soft-shelled clams. Also they eat crabs, crayfish and shrimp. They will also consume isopods and amphipods and fish and worms and some small quantity of soft succulent vegetation. Dr. Archie Carr says that he once fed a thousand diamondbacks on canned war-surplus sardines in tomato sauce. If you have a diamondback and plan to keep it you owe it to yourself and to your pet to read Carr.

Sea Turtles

These are a no-no for hobbyists. Many species are protected and all are difficult to maintain. The eating habits are very specialized and they need a great deal of clean sea water to remain healthy. Some eat jellyfish and others consume large quantities of certain seaweeds. As pets they will give you all sorts of problems with no redeeming features. Incidentally, a large

A female green sea turtle, Chelonia mydas, *on its way back to the sea after laying her eggs out of the water and burying them under the sand.*

leatherback will weigh in at over 1500 pounds, so it becomes the world's heaviest living reptile. This species does have a voice and it is capable of expressing pain and rage.

A group of representative terrestrial turtle species: **facing page:** *(top) juvenile radiated tortoise,* Geochelone radiata, *from Madagascar; (bottom) pancake tortoises,* Malacochersus tornieri, *from Africa;* **this page:** *(right) very young gopher tortoise,* Gopherus polyphemus, *from the United States; and (below) red-footed tortoise,* Geochelone carbonaria, *from South America.*

Terrestrial Turtles

On dry land are the box turtle and gopher and Greek and desert tortoises. The ideal set-up should be based on the kind of land your pet comes from. Gopher tortoises are found in palmetto and pine country while box and wood turtles come from damper eastern woodlands. A wood turtle might even mate in the water, and box turtles are often found bathing or soaking in shallow ponds.

Many of these turtles scavenge for dead animal protein and supplement it with fruits, berries, vegetables and mushrooms. A "V" shaped notch cut in a woodland mushroom is a good indication that a box turtle is nearby.

You may have noticed that the words turtle and tortoise have been interchanged in this chapter. There is no technical difference between tortoise, terrapin and turtle. "Turtle" covers *all* shelled reptiles.

If you choose to keep terrestrial turtles you will find that many are long-lived and easy to maintain. Let's review them briefly.

Gophers: There are but three U.S. species in this family, Testudinidae. Perhaps Theodore Roosevelt lied a little (turtle stories are much like fish stories—they grow in the re-telling) when he said in 1917 that a 13-inch specimen "easily walked away" with Teddy standing on his back. This I believe is unlikely. He also reported that *Gopher polyphemus,* the gopher tortoise of Georgia, South Carolina, Florida, Alabama, Louisiana and Mississippi reaches a carapace length of 18-inches. In 1917 there probably were 18-inch specimens, but today a twelve-inch is a whopper. The other two allied species are *Gopherus agassizi,* the desert tortoise, from southern California and Nevada, south into Mexico, and *G. berlandieri,* Berlandier's tortoise, of southern Texas and contiguous Mexico.

Unfortunately the desert tortoise doesn't do too well in captivity. You would be lucky to keep one always indoors and healthy for even three years. There isn't much data about Berlandier's readily available except that it eats grass but favors more

Keeping a box turtle or some other pet turtle in one's youth is an experience that can not be forgotten.

succulent vegetation. The gopher tortoise, *G. polyphemus,* grows to nine or ten pounds in weight when the carapace calipers one foot. (Not over the curve but in a straight line.) Gophers inhabit long burrows and occupy them with many other animals and insects. These burrows have been excavated by herpetologists, and some extended 35 or even 40 feet. Lately gophers have been protected, and they make poor pets.

If you have a gopher you might feed it Bermuda grass and melon rinds for starters. Of course any turtle wants water both to drink and for an occasional bath.

The genus *Terrapene* (family Emydidae) provides pet keepers with great terrestrial pets; these are the box turtles *Terrapene carolina* and *T. ornata.* Four

In addition to the American box turtles of the genus Terrapene *(T. carolina bauri shown below), the Asiatic genus* Cuora *also provides species commonly known as "box" turtles:* **Facing page:** *(top)* Cuora flavomarginata; *(bottom)* Cuora trifasciata; *and* **this page:** *(right)* American wood turtle, *a terrestrial species but not a box turtle, because its plastron is not hinged.*

or so subspecies of *T. carolina* are recognized. All are attractive and hardy. They are found east of the Great Plains from Florida through the southern half of Maine. *T. ornata* ranges from the Mississippi to the foothills of the Rockies.

A hinged plastron permits the box turtle to close up fore and aft so tightly that a matchstick cannot be wedged in. This will rarely happen with a captive specimen, since most of them grow too fat to pull everything in at the same time. If the front is closed, the rear must remain open and *vice versa.*
Box turtles make good inside or outside pets. Provide them with a garden mulch pile for hibernation and they may voluntarily remain with you for years with little or no restraint. Conant mentions twenty-three years of captivity for a box turtle, and others tell us that a life span of 100 years is reasonable to expect.

Lettuce, bananas, apple, melons, mushrooms and chopped beef (raw or cooked) are all favored foods.

Still another U.S. species of this large family found in damp woodlands is the wood turtle, *Clemmys insculpta*. It has handsomely "sculptured"

carapace shields from which it derives its scientific name. The plastron is not hinged. The wood turtle makes a great pet so long as it is not protected by law where you capture it or where you plan to keep it. It needs to be in or close to water. Pet keepers consider it to have a superior intelligence among turtles. In my experience, only the diamondback comes close to it. Wood turtles are found in Nova Scotia and throughout all of New England, south to Virginia and west (irregularly) to Wisconsin. A large wood turtle will be just under nine inches carapace length. With its sculptured carapace and orange throat and lower limb surfaces, it is easy to recognize.

This turtle adapts itself to your home, your garden, a bog or even a relatively dry woodland. It is a great pet. It will eat any raw, unspiced food you eat and a great deal more besides.

Wood turtles are said to whistle when they make love; well, maybe. We do know, however, that they copulate in the water.

One more terrestrial turtle that favors wet places is the protected, rare and elusive Muhlenberg's turtle.

Specimens of the Moorish tortoise, Testudo graeca, *a popular species in Europe occasionally reach the United States. They normally hibernate during winter.*

Clemmys muhlenbergi looks like a wood turtle without the deep sculpturing. The carapace of an adult is only four inches long. The outstanding feature for recognition of this species is the orange blotch on each side of its head. The carapace is not spotted. The plastron is notched under the tail and is not hinged.

Muhlenberg's turtle is found in bogs in North Carolina, Virginia, northern Maryland, eastern Pennsylvania and New Jersey,

Many turtle species are unfit for keeping by even experienced fanciers. Some are overly delicate, some require special care, some are endangered and therefore illegal to keep—or all three elements of unsuitability combined. **Facing page:** (top) Chelonia depressa and (bottom) Eretmochelys imbricata are sea turtles that would be difficult to keep even if they weren't endangered, and **this page** (above) Geochelone elephantopus is a giant tortoise from the Galapagos that can weigh over 500 pounds.

western and southern New York and extreme western Connecticut, but an avid herpetologist could spend years looking unless he had help from someone who already knew. This species eats on land and also under water. It has been known to consume earthworms and berries, but it is really so small and elusive and spottily distributed that we really don't know much about it. The turtle is endangered, so for legal and conservation reasons it should not be collected or kept captive.

The Mediterranean land turtles *Testudo hermanni,* the Greek or Hermann's tortoise, and *T. graeca,* the Moorish, Iberian, or spur-thighed tortoise, are long-time favorites of pet keepers. *Testudo graeca* erroneously has been called the "Greek" tortoise before. Treat either of them as you would a box or gopher tortoise. Each of these is actually represented by several similar species or subspecies and all make great pets in the terrarium or in the garden.

If you wish to learn more about these European forms, read Pritchard. Briefly, *T.*

hermanni is long-lived, and specimens have been kept captive for 100 years. They are nearly 100% vegetarian and many seem to favor a diet of yellow-colored flowers. The largest European *Testudo* might measure one foot. Most are much smaller.

Another genus of land turtles (commonly called tortoises) is *Geochelone,* and representatives are found in Africa, South America, the Far East, and on Pacific and Indian Ocean Islands with romantic sounding names like Galapagos, Seychelles, Celebes, Madagascar and Aldabra. They are mostly large species. Some are protected because they're endangered; some are virtually extinct. Remember, if you ever should obtain one of these, that they are nearly 100% vegetarian and love sunlight but deserve shade. They need dryness to protect against fungus infection, but they must have clean fresh drinking water available; for most, the ideal temperature would be between 75° F. and 85° F. Those species that are native to rainforests need more moisture than do the forms from desert islands.

Index

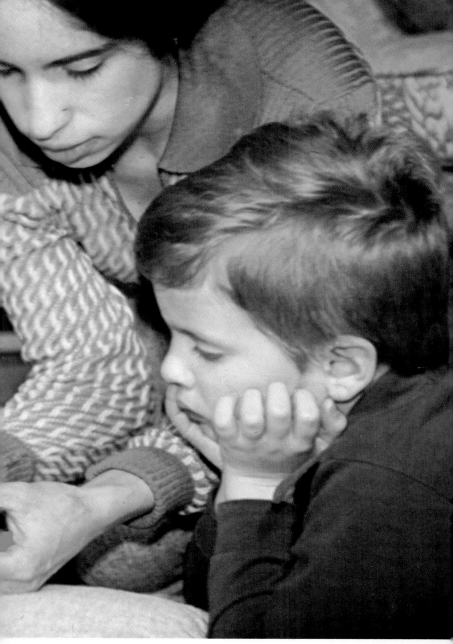

TURTLES
KW-051